Etsy Empress: Crafting a Profitable Passion

Table of Contents

Chapter 1: Introduction: The Etsy Phenomenon

Etsy: it's not just another online marketplace. Since its inception in 2005, it has blossomed into the go-to hub for unique, handmade, vintage, and craft supplies, connecting passionate makers with eager buyers from all over the world. Let's delve into the captivating journey of Etsy and discover why it's a haven for craftpreneurs.

The Birth and Rise of Etsy

In the bustling Brooklyn neighborhood of New York City, Etsy was born from a simple idea: there needed to be a dedicated platform for craftsmen and artists to sell their creations. Unlike massive online retailers, Etsy's vision was to focus on the personal, the unique, and the artisanal.

In the early days, Etsy was like a digital craft fair, attracting sellers who found its ethos appealing. But what really set Etsy apart was its commitment to community. Here, sellers were not just anonymous storefronts but real people, each with a story to tell about their creations. This approach resonated deeply with shoppers looking for something different from mass-produced items. As a result, Etsy's growth was organic, fueled by word-of-mouth and the sheer passion of its community.

Now, consider this: in its first year, Etsy had sales of around $170,000. Fast forward to recent years, and the platform has facilitated billions in sales annually. The secret? Fostering a unique ecosystem where creativity is celebrated, and the handmade has immense value.

Why Etsy is a Craftpreneur's Paradise

The digital age has presented endless opportunities for entrepreneurs. However, for artists and crafters, traditional e-commerce platforms often felt impersonal and overwhelming. Etsy bridged this gap brilliantly. Here's why:

1. Community-Oriented: On Etsy, you're not just a seller; you're a member of a global community. The platform is designed to foster connections, not just transactions. Through forums, teams, and local events, Etsy sellers have myriad opportunities to collaborate, learn, and grow.

2. Niche Audience: Etsy buyers aren't looking for the generic. They come to Etsy for the personal touch, the story behind an item, the human connection. If you've got a unique product or story, you'll find an audience eager to listen and buy.

3. Brand Identity: Unlike other platforms where you're just another seller, Etsy allows you to craft a distinct shop identity. From your shop's banner, logo, to the story section, you can showcase your brand's personality. Remember, buyers don't just buy a product; they buy the story, the brand, and the person behind it.

4. Seller Tools: Etsy continually rolls out tools to aid sellers in managing and optimizing their shops. From detailed analytics to marketing tools and integrative shipping solutions, Etsy has made it relatively seamless to run a shop, even if you're a newbie.

5. Global Reach with a Local Feel: No matter where you are in the world, when you set up an Etsy shop, you gain access to a global customer base. Yet, the platform maintains a "local craft fair" vibe, giving sellers the best of both worlds.

Golden Nugget: The power of Etsy lies in its authenticity. In an age where everything is digitized and automated, shoppers are increasingly craving genuine human connection and unique products that have a story. As an Etsy seller, you're not just offering a product; you're offering a piece of yourself, your passion, and your creativity. And there lies the true magic of the platform.

As we delve deeper into this guide, we'll uncover the tools, strategies, and insights that will help you navigate Etsy's vibrant landscape and transform your passion into a thriving online business. The world is eager for your creations; let's help them discover you on Etsy.

Chapter 2: Setting Up for Success: Your Etsy Shop Basics

Starting an Etsy shop is much more than just listing products and waiting for sales. It's about creating a brand, an experience, and a connection with your audience. Let's explore the foundational elements of a successful Etsy store and how you can make a lasting impression from the start.

Crafting Your Shop's Unique Identity

Before you dive into the technicalities of setting up your store, take a moment to envision your brand. Your shop's identity is the first thing potential customers will interact with. It can differentiate you in a crowded marketplace and make you memorable.

1. Shop Name: It should resonate with what you sell but also be catchy and memorable. Avoid using overly generic names. If you're selling handmade candles, "Luminous Creations" might be more captivating than "Mary's Candles."

2. Logo & Banner: Invest time (or even a little money) in a professional-looking logo. This isn't just about aesthetics; it's about brand recognition. Platforms like Canva or hiring a freelancer on Fiverr can yield fantastic results. Your banner, meanwhile, offers a larger canvas to communicate your brand's essence, perhaps showcasing your products or a behind-the-scenes snapshot of your crafting process.

3. About Section: Here's where the magic happens! Tell your story. Why did you start crafting? What's the story behind your brand? Sharing personal anecdotes or inspirations can create a bond between you and your potential buyer.

Tip: Customers love behind-the-scenes content. Consider adding a photo of your workspace, or a short video of you creating. It humanizes your brand and makes customers feel they're buying from a real person with passion and expertise.

Understanding Etsy's Fees and Guidelines

Etsy provides a wonderful platform for sellers, but it's crucial to understand the costs involved to ensure profitability. Here's a breakdown:

1. Listing Fees: Etsy charges a fee for every item you list. It's a nominal amount, but it can add up, especially if you have many products.

2. Transaction Fees: When you make a sale, Etsy takes a percentage of the total sale amount, including shipping.

3. Payment Processing Fees: If you use Etsy Payments (and it's recommended for the ease of your customers), there's a fee for processing each transaction.

4. Offsite Ads Fees: If Etsy advertises your products outside of their platform and it results in a sale, you will be charged an advertising fee. While this can increase visibility and sales, be sure to factor this into your pricing strategy.

5. Other Fees: This might include currency conversion, in-person selling fees, or fees related to Pattern (Etsy's website-building tool).

Before listing products, familiarize yourself with Etsy's Seller Policy and House Rules. These guidelines ensure the platform remains trusted and genuine. For instance, you should know what items are prohibited or what the guidelines are around handmade vs. vintage vs. craft supplies.

Tip: When factoring in Etsy's fees, also consider other costs like shipping supplies, packaging, and any tools or software you might use to manage your shop. This will ensure you price your items in a way that protects your profit margins.

Getting started on Etsy is exhilarating, but the initial setup is more than a logistical step; it's laying the foundation for your brand's future. With a clear identity and an understanding of Etsy's landscape, you position yourself not just as another seller, but as a memorable brand that stands out. The next chapters will guide you through finding your niche, product sourcing, and mastering the art of listings, setting you on a trajectory for Etsy success.

Chapter 3: Discovering Your Etsy Niche

Identifying Trending Crafts and Designs

Etsy is a vibrant marketplace with countless products vying for attention. To succeed, you need to discover what's trending while remaining true to your own creative passion. So, how can you identify these trends?

1. Etsy Trending Items: Start with Etsy itself! The platform often showcases trending items on its homepage. These can provide insight into what shoppers are currently craving.

2. Social Media & Pinterest: Platforms like Instagram and Pinterest are hotbeds of creative inspiration. Search for craft and design hashtags or explore popular boards to see what styles or products are gaining traction.

3. Etsy Seller Forums: This is a community of sellers just like you, discussing challenges, successes, and insights. Keep an eye out for threads discussing best-selling items or emerging trends.

4. Trade Shows & Craft Fairs: These events can offer a first-hand look at what's becoming popular. Plus, interacting directly with other creators can spark innovative ideas for your own shop.

Tip: Set up Google Alerts for terms related to your craft. This way, you'll receive updates about emerging trends, ensuring you're always one step ahead of the curve.

The Importance of Authenticity and Originality

While it's essential to know what's trending, it's equally crucial to infuse your unique touch into everything you create. Here's why:

1. Stand Out in a Crowded Market: There might be thousands of jewelry sellers on Etsy, but your unique design or story can make your brand memorable.

2. Build a Loyal Customer Base: Customers are more likely to return to a shop that offers something they can't find elsewhere. Originality creates that magnetic pull.

3. Personal Fulfillment: At the end of the day, many sellers are on Etsy because they love their craft. Staying true to yourself ensures that passion doesn't wane.

How to Infuse Authenticity into Your Products:

1. Narrative: Each product should have a story. Whether it's about the inspiration behind the design, the sourcing of materials, or the crafting process, these narratives draw buyers in.

2. Signature Touch: Consider what can be your trademark. Maybe it's a particular material, a specific design flourish, or even the packaging. This touch will set your product apart.

3. Engage Directly with Your Audience: Use your shop updates, social media, or blog posts to share your journey, mistakes, successes, and lessons. It makes your brand more relatable and human.

Tip: Host a monthly 'Behind-The-Scenes' day on platforms like Instagram. Showcase your crafting process, share sneak peeks of new products, or share your workspace. It's a fun way to engage your audience and reinforce your brand's authenticity.

Navigating the fine line between trending designs and originality is an art. However, by staying informed about market demands while never losing sight of your unique voice, you can create an Etsy store that's both popular and personal. As we venture into the intricacies of product creation and sourcing in the next chapter, remember: your unique touch is your ultimate USP (Unique Selling Proposition)!

Chapter 4: Product Creation and Sourcing

Handmade Wonders: Crafting Best Practices

Crafting by hand brings a certain charm to your Etsy products that can't be replicated by mass-produced items. But how do you ensure that every piece you create meets the highest standards?

1. Consistency: While every handmade item will have its unique quirks, strive for consistent quality. This means using templates or molds for repetitive designs, ensuring similar product sizes, colors, and features.

2. Materials: Source the best materials you can afford. High-quality materials not only enhance your product's appeal but also its longevity. Whether it's a special type of fabric, organic yarn, or a unique gemstone, your materials can elevate your product's perceived value.

3. Continuous Learning: Craftsmanship improves over time. Attend workshops, watch tutorials, and practice, practice, practice. The more skilled you become, the more intricate and valued your products can be.

Tip: Consider creating a limited edition series once in a while. By using a unique material or technique, you can attract buyers looking for something special.

Partnering with Artisans and Suppliers

While handcrafting items yourself has its merits, as you scale up, you might consider partnering with other artisans or finding suppliers. Here's how:

1. Local Artisan Collaborations: Teaming up with a local artisan can give your products a fresh twist. For instance, if you make ceramic mugs, collaborating with a local painter for designs can set your mugs apart.

2. Finding Reliable Suppliers: If you use components that you don't make yourself, like chains for handmade pendants, ensure you source from reputable suppliers.

Check reviews, order samples, and establish a good relationship with them.

3. Ethical Sourcing: More buyers today value ethically sourced products. If you're using natural materials, ensure they're sustainably harvested. If you're buying from artisans, ensure they're paid fairly.

Tip: Include the story of your suppliers or collaborators in your product description. For example, if your wool is sourced from a particular farm or community, share their story. It adds depth to your product's narrative and resonates with ethically-minded consumers.

Crafting vs. Outsourcing Decisions

As you grow, you'll face the decision: Do I craft this myself or outsource it?

1. Skillset Evaluation: Be honest about what you excel in and what might be done better (or faster) by someone else. If beading isn't your strength but is essential for your designs, outsourcing could be a wise choice.

2. Time Management: If crafting a particular item takes too long, reducing your potential product output, consider if outsourcing parts of the process would be more efficient.

3. Cost Analysis: Sometimes, buying a component can be cheaper than making it yourself, without compromising quality. Do the math.

Tip: If you decide to outsource, always order a sample first. This ensures the product meets your standards before placing a larger order.

Remember, the essence of Etsy is the personal touch and the story behind each product. Whether you're handcrafting every item or partnering with artisans and suppliers, ensure that the heart and soul of your brand shine through in every piece. It's this authenticity, combined with quality craftsmanship, that will set your Etsy shop apart.

Chapter 5: The Art of the Etsy Listing

Photography: Capturing Your Craft's Best Angle

The moment a potential buyer lands on your Etsy listing, the first thing that grabs their attention is the product photo. Think of it as the window display of your virtual store.

1. Professional Lighting: Even if you don't have professional equipment, natural lighting can work wonders. Position your products near a large window, preferably during early morning or late afternoon for the softest light.

2. Background Matters: Use neutral backgrounds like white or soft pastels to make your product stand out. If relevant, use props, but ensure they don't overshadow the product.

3. Multiple Angles: Showcase your product from various angles. Close-ups can highlight intricate details, while wider shots can give a sense of scale.

4. Consistency: Keeping a consistent style across all product photos builds brand identity. This means maintaining the same light quality, background, and editing style.

Tip: For a more interactive experience, consider adding a short video to your listing. It gives buyers a 360-degree view and a better feel for the product.

Crafting Titles and Descriptions That Sell

Once your photo reels them in, your title and description should seal the deal.

1. Clear and Descriptive Titles: While it's tempting to use flowery language, clarity trumps all. If you're selling a "Hand-painted Ceramic Teacup," say just that. Avoid vague titles like "Gorgeous Handmade Drinkware."

2. Optimize for Etsy Search: Include essential keywords in your title. If you're unsure about which keywords to use, think about what terms you'd type into the search bar if you were looking for your product.

3. Engaging Descriptions: Start with the most important details: size, materials, colors, and care instructions. Then, delve into the story behind the product. Was it inspired by a trip to the mountains? Or maybe it's a family design passed down through generations? Personal stories can create an emotional connection.

4. Address Potential Concerns: Think about common questions buyers might have. Is the ring size adjustable? Can the fabric be machine washed? Answering these upfront can reduce back-and-forth messaging and increase buyer confidence.

Tip: Use bullet points or short paragraphs in your description. Big blocks of text can be daunting and are often skipped over.

Making the Most of Tags and Categories

Etsy allows you to add tags to your listing, which can help potential buyers find your product when they search.

1. Relevant Tags: Think like your buyer. Which terms or phrases might they use? If you're selling a wooden cutting board, potential tags could be "kitchenware," "handcrafted wood," "chopping board," and "gift for cooks."

2. Avoid Overly Generic Tags: While "gift" might be relevant, it's too broad. "Birthday gift for her" or "anniversary gift for husband" are more targeted and effective.

3. Utilize All Tags: Etsy allows 13 tags. Use them all. Even if you feel you've covered the main ones, think outside the box and use up all available tags to maximize your listing's reach.

Tip: Look at competitors with similar products. Don't copy, but let their tags inspire you. If they consistently use a tag you hadn't thought of, consider its relevance to your product.

Your Etsy listing is the gateway to your shop. Combining captivating photos with compelling titles, descriptions, and savvy tagging will not only attract more visitors but convert them into loyal customers. Remember, every detail matters in the digital marketplace – make each one count!

Chapter 6: Etsy Pricing and Profit Margins

Competing on Price vs. Value

Setting the right price for your product is a balancing act. While you might be tempted to set a lower price to attract more buyers, it's essential to ensure that the price reflects the value of your product.

1. Know Your Market: Study competitors with similar products. Are you offering something extra that could justify a slightly higher price?

2. Perceived Value: Incorporate elements that elevate the perceived value of your product. This could be anything from exclusive designs, high-quality materials, or limited edition items. When buyers see added value, they are more willing to pay a premium.

3. Psychological Pricing: Ever wondered why products are priced at $19.99 instead of $20? It's because prices ending in .99 often feel cheaper to buyers. Consider employing this tactic, but use it judiciously.

Tip: Occasionally, offer limited-time discounts to attract fence-sitters without devaluing your products.

Understanding Costs: Materials, Labor, and Overhead

Before you can set a profitable price, you need to have a clear understanding of your costs. Overlooking any aspect could mean the difference between profit and loss.

1. Materials: Make a detailed list of every material used. If you make jewelry, this includes not just the main elements like gemstones or metal but also clasps, strings, and even packaging.

2. Labor: Determine how long it takes to make one item and decide on a fair hourly wage for yourself. Multiply the two, and you've got your labor cost.

3. Overhead: This can be tricky. Remember to account for things like electricity (if you work from a home studio), Etsy's listing and transaction fees, tools, and equipment depreciation.

4. Profit Margin: Once you've tallied up your costs, decide on a profit margin. This shouldn't be an arbitrary number. Think about the growth and sustainability of your business. A good starting point for handmade items can be a keystone pricing strategy, where the retail price is double your total costs.

Tip: Use spreadsheet software to track your costs. This way, you can easily update it if material prices change, and it can help you analyze your most and least profitable products.

Future-proofing Your Pricing

The market is dynamic, and so are your costs. Regularly revisit your pricing strategy.

1. Account for Seasonality: Some products, especially handmade ones, can demand higher prices during peak seasons. For instance, knitted scarves might sell for more in winter than in summer.

2. Factor in Sales and Discounts: If you plan on having a sale, ensure that your regular prices can accommodate these discounts and still remain profitable.

3. Survey Your Customers: Occasionally, ask your customers if they feel they're getting value for their money. This feedback can be a goldmine.

4. Stay Updated with Market Trends: The demand for products can fluctuate based on trends. If a particular style or product becomes highly sought-after, consider adjusting your prices accordingly.

Tip: Consider introducing a loyalty program or exclusive discounts for repeat customers. This not only boosts sales but also encourages buyers to provide regular feedback, helping you stay attuned to their perceptions about your pricing.

Pricing isn't just about covering costs; it's an art that requires understanding your market, your customers, and the unique value proposition of your products. Set your prices with confidence, and remember that you're not just selling an item, but a story, a craft, and an experience.

Chapter 7: Building Trust: Customer Service and Reviews

Effective Communication with Buyers

In an online marketplace where buyers don't have the luxury of seeing products in person, effective communication becomes paramount. You're not just selling products; you're selling trust.

1. Transparency: Always be clear about what the buyer is purchasing. Mention specifics – sizes, colors, materials, and anything else pertinent. This reduces confusion and the chances of returns.

2. Responsiveness: Try to reply to messages and queries as soon as possible. This doesn't mean you need to be glued to your computer, but setting specific times during the day to check and respond can be a game-changer.

3. Custom Orders: If you're open to customization, make it clear. Buyers love items tailored to their preferences, and it could lead to higher sales. Remember to adjust pricing and communicate timelines accordingly.

Tip: Consider setting up an FAQ section addressing common questions. It saves time for both you and the potential buyer.

Dealing with Returns, Refunds, and Negative Feedback

No matter how hard you try, not every transaction will go perfectly. But handling imperfections well can set you apart.

1. Clear Return Policies: Before a purchase, customers should know your stance on returns. Is it a 30-day return window? Do they pay for return shipping? Be specific, but also considerate.

2. Handle Issues Promptly: If a buyer has a problem, address it swiftly. The quicker a resolution, the more likely they'll leave a positive review despite the hiccup.

3. Feedback is Gold: Negative feedback, while hurtful, can be constructive. If someone wasn't happy with the product or service, see it as an opportunity to improve. Thank them for their input and consider making necessary adjustments.

Tip: If a negative review is due to a shipping error or something out of your control, address it professionally in the comments. Future buyers will see that you're proactive and care about customer satisfaction.

Reviews: The Backbone of Trust

A glowing review can mean more to your store's success than the most polished advertisement.

1. Encourage Reviews: After a purchase, send a thank-you note and kindly ask for a review. Many buyers forget, but a gentle nudge can do wonders.

2. Offer Incentives: Consider offering a small discount on the next purchase for leaving a review. However, always ensure it doesn't come off as "buying" a positive review.

3. Showcase Your Best Reviews: Use social media or even your Etsy store banner to highlight some of the best feedback you've received. It's social proof at its finest.

Tip: Engage with your positive reviews too! Thanking a satisfied customer publicly reinforces your image as an attentive and appreciative seller.

Building trust isn't just about making a sale; it's about forging lasting relationships with your customer base. By prioritizing clear communication, addressing concerns head-on, and celebrating feedback, you're laying down the foundation for a successful, long-term Etsy enterprise. And always remember: In the world of online shopping, trust isn't just a bonus; it's currency

Chapter 8: Etsy's Search Algorithm and SEO

Keywords, Tags, and Titles: Etsy SEO Explained

Understanding Etsy's search algorithm is akin to unlocking the secret door to your shop for potential buyers. SEO, or Search Engine Optimization, isn't just for Google – it's vital for Etsy sellers too.

1. Keyword Research: Before listing, take some time to research keywords related to your product. Free tools like EtsyRank can give you a sense of what shoppers are looking for. Think about what potential buyers would type in to find your product.

2. Optimize Titles: Begin your product title with the most crucial keyword. However, ensure it still reads naturally. For instance, instead of "Silver Necklace Star-shaped," consider "Star-shaped Silver Necklace."

3. Use All 13 Tags: Etsy allows 13 tags for your listing, and it's wise to use them all. Think of synonyms, local spellings (e.g., 'color' and 'colour'), and related terms.

4. Category Matters: Be specific with the category and attributes (like size or color) you choose for your listing. It can make a world of difference in helping your item appear in relevant searches.

Tip: Think like a buyer. If you were searching for your product, what terms would you use? Even better, ask a friend or family member unfamiliar with your product to describe it; they might use terms you hadn't considered.

Riding the Trend Waves: Seasonal and Event-Based SEO

Trends and seasons can significantly influence shopping behaviors, and savvy Etsy sellers can use this to their advantage.

1. Holiday & Seasonal Keywords: If Christmas is coming, and you have relevant products, incorporate seasonal keywords like "Christmas gift," "holiday decor," or "winter wear."

2. Event-based SEO: Beyond holidays, think of events like weddings, graduations, baby showers, or even pop culture happenings. For instance, during popular TV show releases, related keywords might spike.

3. Track Trend Reports: Etsy often releases trend reports, offering insights into what buyers are currently interested in. Stay updated and pivot your listings when necessary.

4. Update Listings: Just because you've set your keywords once doesn't mean they're set in stone. Regularly revisit and update them based on trends, seasons, and new insights.

Tip: Create a calendar of events, holidays, and potential trends for the year. Plan and adjust your SEO strategies around these dates. For instance, search interest for "Halloween costumes" typically begins to rise in September.

Remember, while SEO can significantly improve visibility, it's essential to combine it with high-quality products and excellent customer service. Moreover, always ensure your listing accurately represents your product. Misleading buyers with irrelevant keywords can lead to dissatisfaction and negative reviews.

The world of Etsy SEO is ever-evolving, with the platform regularly updating its algorithm. But by understanding its core principles and adapting to trends and seasons, you position your shop at the forefront, ready to capture the attention of eager buyers. The combination of well-researched keywords and trend awareness can be a game-changer, potentially elevating your store from hidden gem to Etsy hotspot.

Chapter 9: Promoting Your Etsy Store

Utilizing Etsy Ads and Promotions

To boost your shop's visibility, consider Etsy's built-in advertising solutions. These tools can help you appear more prominently in search results or gain exposure on other platforms.

1. Etsy Ads: By setting a daily budget, you can push your listings to appear at the top of Etsy search results. However, be strategic. Ensure the products you promote are best-sellers or have unique appeal to maximize ROI.

2. Etsy Offsite Ads: These ads showcase your products on sites like Google, Facebook, and Instagram. You only pay when someone clicks the ad and buys from your shop. Monitor performance and adjust budgets as necessary.

3. Run Sales and Promotions: Limited-time discounts can lure hesitant buyers. Utilize Etsy's "Sales and Coupons" feature to offer deals like free shipping or percentage off.

Tip: Start with a modest ad budget. Monitor performance closely, understanding which products yield the best results, and adjust your budget accordingly.

Cross-Promotion on Social Media and Blogs

Expanding your reach beyond Etsy can exponentially increase your potential customer base.

1. Social Media Presence: Platforms like Instagram and Pinterest are visual-centric, perfect for showcasing handcrafted products. Use high-quality images, engage with followers, and use relevant hashtags. Regular posts, stories, and reels can help maintain visibility.

2. Collaborate with Bloggers: Identify niche bloggers whose audience aligns with your products. Send them a sample for review or sponsor a post. Their endorsement can bring a stream of new customers.

3. Email Newsletters: Collect email addresses (ethically) and send newsletters showcasing new products, behind-the-scenes peeks, and exclusive deals. Tools like Mailchimp make this process smooth.

Tip: Use tools like Linktree on platforms like Instagram, where you can't use direct links in posts. This way, potential buyers can access your Etsy shop, blog, and other platforms through a single link.

Collaborations and Partnering with Influencers

In today's digital age, influencers wield significant power. Collaborating can lead to exposure to vast audiences overnight.

1. Identify Relevant Influencers: Not all influencers will be a good fit. Find those whose style and audience align with your products.

2. Send PR Packages: An unsolicited, beautifully-packaged product can catch an influencer's eye. It's no guarantee, but if they love it, they might share it, leading to organic promotion.

3. Paid Collaborations: For guaranteed exposure, consider paying influencers for a post or story. Always clarify terms, such as how and when the product will be showcased.

Tip: Engage with influencers before reaching out. Genuine comments on their posts can put you on their radar, making them more receptive when you propose a collaboration.

Promotion, when done strategically, can skyrocket your Etsy shop's success. It's not just about casting the net wide but ensuring you're reaching the right audience with compelling content. Whether through ads, social media, or influencers, give potential buyers a reason to click on your store and, more importantly, make a purchase. A dynamic, multi-platform promotional strategy can be the difference between a hobbyist seller and a thriving Etsy entrepreneur.

Chapter 10: Shipping and Fulfillment Strategies

Packaging with a Personal Touch

Etsy shoppers aren't just buying a product; they're purchasing an experience. Your packaging can be the cherry on top that sets your store apart from the rest.

1. Branded Packaging: Invest in custom stickers, labels, or even personalized boxes. Not only does this look professional, but it also boosts brand recall.

2. Thank You Notes: A small handwritten thank you note can go a long way. It adds a personal touch, making customers feel valued and more likely to return or leave a positive review.

3. Protective Packaging: While aesthetic is crucial, function is paramount. Ensure that fragile items are securely wrapped and won't break during transit.

Tip: Consider using eco-friendly packaging. Many consumers appreciate sustainable options, and it can be a unique selling point for your store.

International Shipping: What to Know

Shipping worldwide can dramatically increase your customer base. However, it comes with its own set of challenges.

1. Research Shipping Costs: Before offering international shipping, understand the costs. Websites like USPS, FedEx, or DHL can give you estimates based on weight and destination.

2. Customs and Duties: Some countries might impose customs duties on imported goods. It's essential to communicate to buyers that they might have to pay additional charges upon arrival.

3. Transit Time: International shipping can take weeks. Clearly mention expected delivery times to manage customer expectations.

Tip: Offer a premium shipping option. Some international customers are willing to pay more for faster delivery.

Streamlining and Automating Order Fulfillment

As orders increase, streamlining becomes essential to maintain efficiency and customer satisfaction.

1. Batch Processing: Instead of handling orders one by one, set specific days/times for order processing. This helps in organizing and often leads to quicker fulfillment.

2. Inventory Management Tools: Platforms like Craftybase or QuickBooks can help track your products, materials, and expenses. Knowing your inventory can prevent overselling and backorders.

3. Shipping Label Printers: Invest in a dedicated label printer. It speeds up the packing process and ensures that addresses are clear and legible, reducing chances of lost mail.

4. Outsource or Use Fulfillment Centers: If you're overwhelmed with orders, consider using fulfillment centers or hiring help. They can store, pack, and ship orders on your behalf.

Tip: If you're considering hiring or outsourcing, start during peak seasons (like holidays) to test the waters. If it works, you can make it a permanent part of your business model.

Shipping can make or break an Etsy business. Late or damaged deliveries can lead to negative reviews, so it's crucial to prioritize this aspect of your business. Remember, it's not just about getting the product to the customer but ensuring the entire process, from ordering to unboxing, is smooth and memorable. The more you streamline and add personal touches to your shipping and fulfillment process, the more you set yourself up for success and repeat business.

Chapter 11: Scaling and Expanding Beyond Etsy

When to Hire or Outsource

As your Etsy shop grows, handling every aspect can become overwhelming. Recognizing when to delegate can be the key to maintaining growth without compromising on quality.

1. Tasks Not Your Strength: Whether it's accounting, social media marketing, or photography, if it's not your strong suit, consider hiring an expert. They can bring in a fresh perspective and professionalism.

2. Time-Consuming Tasks: Packing and shipping, for instance, might eat up a lot of your time. By outsourcing, you can focus on product creation and other revenue-generating activities.

3. Cost-Benefit Analysis: Before hiring, always weigh the costs against the benefits. If hiring someone can boost your sales or reduce errors significantly, it's worth the investment.

Insight: Some Etsy sellers bring in virtual assistants (VAs) for specific tasks like customer service or listing management. Platforms like Upwork or Fiverr can be great starting points to find a VA tailored to your needs.

Exploring Other Online Marketplaces

Etsy is fantastic, but there's a world of opportunity out there. Diversifying can increase your reach and reduce dependency on one platform.

1. Amazon Handmade: It's Amazon's answer to Etsy, offering artisans a platform to sell handmade goods to Amazon's massive customer base.

2. eBay: Although known for auctions, eBay's "Buy It Now" feature is ideal for handmade and craft items.

3. Shopify or BigCommerce: These platforms can help you create your standalone store. While it requires more marketing effort, it gives you more control.

Tip: If you're branching out, ensure brand consistency across platforms. It aids in brand recognition and trust.

Building Your Own E-commerce Website

Having your own website gives you complete control and reduces dependency on third-party platforms that can change their rules or take a cut from your profits.

1. Domain Name: Choose a memorable and relevant domain name. It's an essential aspect of your brand identity.

2. Website Builders: Platforms like Wix, WordPress with WooCommerce, or Squarespace are user-friendly and offer e-commerce functionalities.

3. Customization: Your website should reflect your brand. Play with colors, themes, and layouts that match your products and ethos.

4. Email Marketing Integration: Capture visitor emails. Platforms like Mailchimp or SendinBlue can help you set up newsletters, promoting return visits and sales.

Insight: With tools like Google Analytics, you can gain deep insights into your visitors' behavior on your site, allowing for refined marketing strategies and better product placements.

Challenges and Solutions: Owning a website means you're responsible for driving traffic. SEO, Pay-per-click advertising, and social media promotion become even more crucial. However, every penny and effort invested goes back into growing your independent brand.

Remember, while Etsy is a great starting point, having multiple sales channels can increase your brand's resilience against market changes. It's like the old saying, "Don't put all your eggs in one basket." By diversifying your sales platforms and expanding beyond Etsy, you not only tap into a broader audience but also build a stronger, more sustainable business foundation.

Chapter 12: Staying Updated and Inspired

Adapting to Etsy's Changing Algorithms and Policies

Etsy, like all online platforms, evolves. Changes to its search algorithms or policies can impact your store's visibility and sales.

1. Stay Informed: Regularly check Etsy's Seller Handbook and official forums. This ensures you're among the first to know about any updates.

2. Be Flexible: Don't be afraid to tweak your strategies based on new changes. This can involve adjusting product listings, tags, or even prices.

3. Engage with the Community: Join Etsy seller groups on social media. They can be a treasure trove of shared experiences and insights on adapting to changes.

Insight: Etsy often tests new features with a select group of sellers. Engaging with the community can give you early insights into what might be coming next.

Joining Etsy Communities and Forums

The Etsy community is a vast network of experienced and novice sellers, all on the same journey as you.

1. Learn from Others: Reading about others' experiences, mistakes, and triumphs can save you time and money. It can also provide you with fresh perspectives.

2. Share Your Experience: Contributing to forums not only builds your reputation but can also lead to collaborative opportunities.

3. Build Relationships: Networking with fellow sellers can lead to collaborations, partnerships, or even bulk deals on materials.

Tip: When joining a new forum or group, take a moment to introduce yourself and your shop. Sharing a personal story about why you started can make you memorable.

Continuing Education: Workshops, Tutorials, and Craft Fairs

Staying updated isn't just about adapting; it's about growing and improving.

1. Online Courses: Platforms like Udemy, Skillshare, or Coursera offer courses on everything from advanced crafting techniques to e-commerce marketing. Investing in learning can directly impact your shop's success.

2. Craft Fairs: Participating or even just attending can be enlightening. You get firsthand feedback, discover new trends, and can even find inspiration for your next bestseller.

3. Tutorials: YouTube and other platforms are filled with crafters sharing their techniques. This is a free and flexible way to learn and gather inspiration.

4. Networking Events: These can introduce you to suppliers, influencers, or even potential business partners.

Insight: Craft fairs aren't just sales opportunities. They can be invaluable learning experiences. Take note of which items attract attention, how other sellers display their products, and what pricing strategies they use.

In the rapidly changing world of e-commerce, standing still is akin to moving backward. Stay curious, be open to new ideas, and remember: Every top Etsy seller was once a beginner. It's their willingness to learn, adapt, and engage that set them apart. Your journey on Etsy is unique, but by staying updated and continually seeking inspiration, you ensure it's also a journey of growth and success.

Chapter 13: Crafting Your Etsy Empire

Reflecting on the Journey: From Hobbyist to Etsy Mogul

Every Etsy success story began with a single idea, a spark. Looking back at your journey can offer not just a sense of accomplishment but also valuable insights.

1. Track Your Milestones: Keep a record of major sales, positive feedback, and shop developments. These act as reminders of your growth and are crucial for adjusting strategies.

2. Regularly Review Feedback: Both positive and negative reviews can serve as a goldmine of information on how to improve your store and offerings.

3. Document Your Journey: Consider keeping a journal or blog about your Etsy journey. This not only serves as personal reflection but can also inspire others, and you might find other craftpreneurs reaching out for collaborations or advice.

Tip: A 'Behind the Scenes' post or video about the making of a popular product can intrigue customers and humanize your brand.

Looking to the Future: Trends, Opportunities, and Growth

The only constant is change. Being proactive in identifying future opportunities is essential to maintaining and scaling your success.

1. Research Future Trends: Stay updated with global design and craft trends. Websites like Pinterest or design magazines can be excellent resources.

2. Diversify Your Product Range: Once you've established a steady customer base, consider introducing new product lines or limited-time offers based on seasonal trends or events.

3. Invest in Technology: From better photography equipment to software that manages inventory and accounts, the right tools can amplify your efficiency and sales.

4. Expand Your Brand: Think about other products or services that align with your brand. Maybe it's time to introduce craft kits, tutorials, or even workshops?

Insight: Etsy's analytics provides a forecast feature showing potential trends. Leverage this to plan your products months in advance.

Lastly, always remember why you started. Was it passion? A desire for financial freedom? Keeping this 'why' at the core of your operations will guide you through challenges and towards greater opportunities.

Every day on Etsy brings new lessons. By staying reflective, proactive, and rooted in your passion, you're not just running an Etsy store; you're crafting an empire. Keep weaving your story, and soon, you might just be the inspiration for a new wave of craftpreneurs.